Our Bodies

Our Muscles

Charlotte Guillain

Heinemann
LIBRARY

www.heinemannlibrary.co.uk
Visit our website to find out more information about Heinemann Library books.

To order:
☎ Phone +44 (0) 1865 888066
🖷 Fax +44 (0) 1865 314091
🖳 Visit www.heinemannlibrary.co.uk

Heinemann Library is an imprint of Capstone Global Library Limited, a company incorporated in England and Wales having its registered office at 7 Pilgrim Street, London, EC4V 6LB – Registered company number: 6695582

Heinemann is a registered trademark of Pearson Education Limited, under licence to Capstone Global Library Limited

Text © Capstone Global Library Limited 2010
First published in hardback in 2010
The moral rights of the proprietor have been asserted.

Edited by Siân Smith, Laura Knowles, Nancy Dickmann, and Rebecca Rissman
Designed by Joanna Hinton-Malivoire
Original Illustrations © Capstone Global Library Ltd. 2010
Illustrated by Tony Wilson
Picture research by Ruth Blair and Mica Brancic
Production by Duncan Gilbert and Victoria Fitzgerald
Originated by Capstone Global Library Ltd
Printed and bound in China by Leo Paper Group

ISBN 978 0 431 19511 7
14 13 12 11 10
10 9 8 7 6 5 4 3 2 1

British Library Cataloguing in Publication Data
Guillain, Charlotte.
  Our muscles. -- (Acorn. Our bodies)
  1. Muscles--Juvenile literature.
  I. Title II. Series
  612.7'4-dc22

Acknowledgements
We would like to thank the following for permission to reproduce photographs: © Capstone Global Library p.**8** (Karon Dubke); Corbis pp.**11** (© David Stoecklein), **20** (© Lisa B.), **22** (© John Lund/Sam Diephuis/Blend Images); iStockphoto pp.**10**, **9** (© Alexander Yakovlev), **17** (© Rosemarie Gearhart); Photolibrary pp.**5** (© HillCreek Pictures BV), **15** (© Rafael Guerrero/Index Stock Imagery), **16** (© OJO Images), **21** (© Banana Stock); Science Photo Library p.**14** (© David Constantine); Shutterstock pp.**13** (© Mandy Godbehear), **18** (© Ostanina Ekaterina Vadimovna).

Front cover photograph of children with hoops reproduced with permission of Corbis (© Randy Faris). Back cover photograph reproduced with permission of iStockphoto.

Every effort has been made to contact copyright holders of material reproduced in this book. Any omissions will be rectified in subsequent printings if notice is given to the publishers.

Community Learning & Libraries
Cymuned Ddysgu a Llyfrgelloedd

This item should be returned or renewed by the
last date stamped below.

---

2 0 NOV 2012

To renew telephone: 656656 or 656657 (minicom)
or www.newport.gov.uk/libraries

ENRICHING
LEARNING IN
NEWPORT
SCHOOLS

Contents

Body parts

Our bodies have many parts.

head

skin

arm

foot

leg

Our bodies have parts on
the outside.

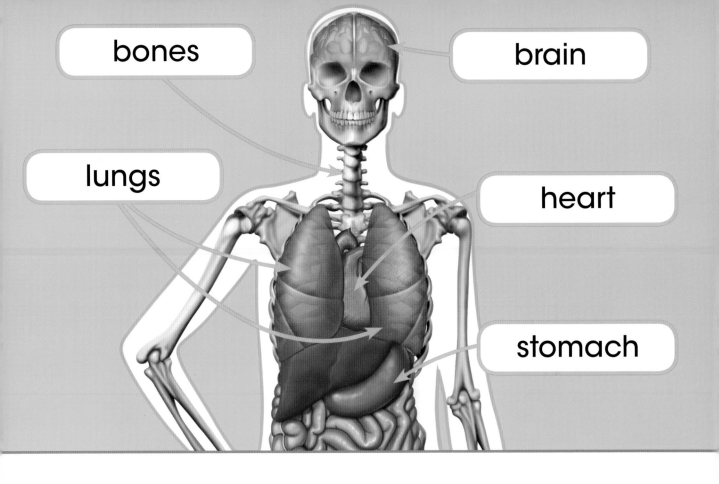

bones

brain

lungs

heart

stomach

Our bodies have parts on the inside.

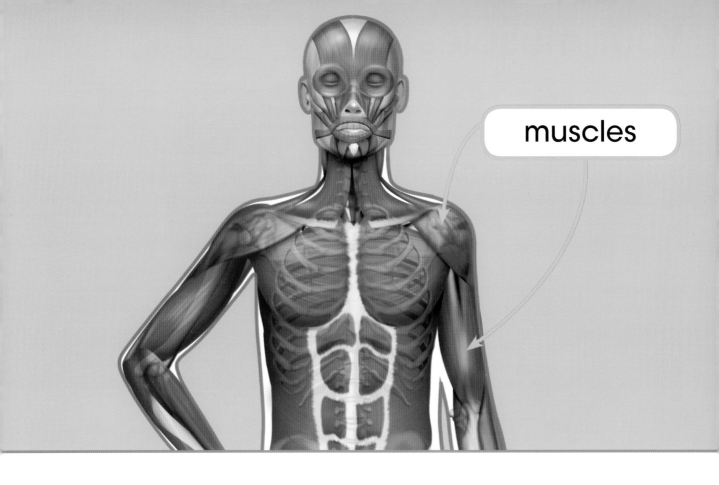

muscles

Your muscles are inside your body.

Your muscles

You cannot see most of
your muscles.

Your muscles are all over your body.

You can feel your muscles.

muscle

You can see the shape of
some muscles.

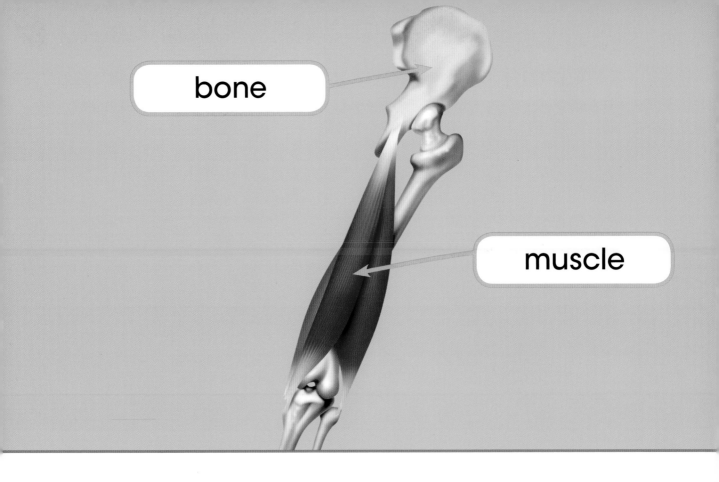

bone

muscle

Some muscles are joined to
your bones.

The muscles pull on your bones to make them move.

What do muscles do?

Your muscles make your body move.

You can choose to move
some muscles.

Some muscles help you
move about.

Some muscles help you smile.

Some muscles work all the time.

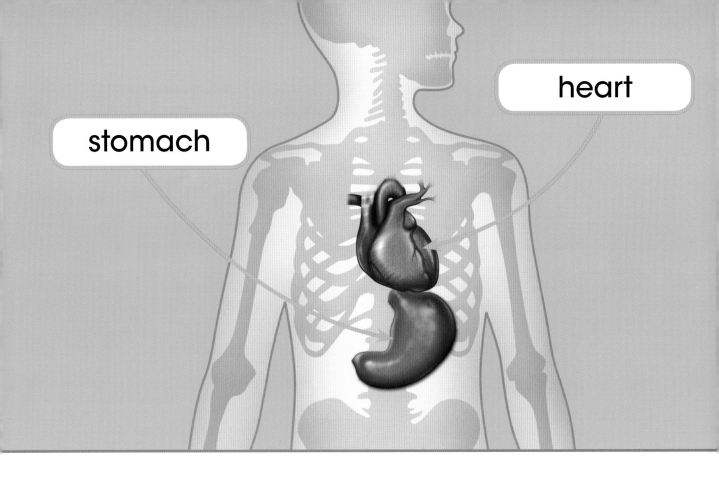

stomach

heart

Your heart and stomach muscles work all the time.

Staying healthy

You can exercise to help
your muscles.

You can eat healthy food to help your muscles.

Quiz

Where in your body are your muscles?

Answer on page 24

Picture glossary

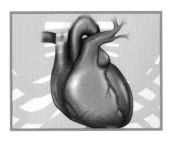

heart a muscle inside your chest. Your heart beats all the time so that it can push blood around your body.

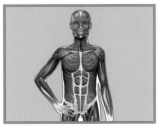

muscles stretchy parts inside your body. Some muscles help you to move your body.

stomach a muscle inside your tummy. Your stomach breaks food into tiny bits so that your body can use it.

Index

Answer to quiz on page 22:
Your muscles are inside your body.

Notes to parents and teachers

Before reading

Ask the children to name the parts of their body they can see on the outside. Then ask them what parts of their body are inside. Make a list of them together and see if the children know what each body part does, for example, food goes into their stomachs. Discuss where their muscles are and see if anyone knows what our muscles are for.

After reading

- Ask the children to step up and down or do jumping jacks for a minute (timed by you). When they have stopped, ask how their legs feel. Discuss how exercise can make our muscles ache and the importance of not straining our muscles.
- Put the children into pairs and ask them to count how many times the other child blinks in a minute (timed by you). Compare the answers and then explain how a muscle in our eyes makes us blink without thinking. Discuss why we need this muscle to work like this.